Huntingdon Area
Middle School Library
Huntingdon, Pa.

Class No. 597.95   Acc. No. 13730

THE GIANT LIZARD

BY SUSAN CREIGHTON

EDITED BY JUDY LOCKWOOD

PUBLISHED BY

CRESTWOOD HOUSE

Mankato, MN, U.S.A.

LIBRARY OF CONGRESS CATALOGING IN PUBLICATION DATA

Creighton, Susan.
  The giant lizard

  (Wildlife, habits & habitat)
  Includes index.
  SUMMARY: Examines the physical characteristics, behavior, lifestyle, and natural environment of the giant monitor lizard.
  1. Monitor lizards—Juvenile literature. [1. Monitor lizards. 2. Lizards] I. Lockwood, Judy. II. Title. III. Series.
  QL666.L29C74   1988   597.95   88-16128
  ISBN 0-89686-394-8

International Standard Book Number:	**Library of Congress Catalog Card Number:**
0-89686-394-8	88-16128

PHOTO CREDITS:

Cover: DRK Photo: D. Cavagnaro
Tom Stack & Associates: (Joe McDonald) 4; (Christopher Crowley) 9; (F.S. Mitchell) 12-13; (Tom Stack) 23
DRK Photo: (Belinda Wright) 7, 24; (R.J. Erwin) 11; (Marty Cordano) 14; (M.P. Kahl) 16; (Stanley Breeden) 19, 21, 33, 35, 39; (C. Allan Morgan) 25, 29, 30, 31, 42-43; (Doug Perrine) 36; (D. Cavagnaro) 27

Copyright© 1988 by Crestwood House, Inc. All rights reserved. No part of this book may be reproduced in any form without written permission from the publisher, except for brief passages included in a review. Printed in the United States of America.
Produced by Carnival Enterprises.

13730

Box 3427, Mankato, MN, U.S.A. 56002

TABLE OF CONTENTS

Introduction: Larger than the average lizard 5
Chapter I: Portrait of the giants 8
    Keen senses and special features
    Jaws and teeth
    Scales cover the monitor
    Useful tails
    Size and life expectancy
Chapter II: Feeding habits 20
    The goanna who lived to eat
    Waiting for prey
    Swallowing the meal
    Some unpleasant habits
    Why cannibalism?
Chapter III: Homes and habitats 30
Chapter IV: The giant lizard in close-up 34
    Courtship, mating, and young
Chapter V: Fierce fights and bad tempers 37
    Battles may lead to death
    The "crazy" monitor
    Not man's best friend
Chapter VI: Giant lizards and man 41
    The most dangerous predator
Map 45
Index/Glossary 46-47

The ancestors of today's giant lizards first appeared on the earth 130 million years ago.

INTRODUCTION:

"When we met him on the trail, he would often advance instead of running away; he'd hiss, open his mouth wide, inflate his throat, and bow his tail and body in a threatening posture."

A monster, you say? Maybe a dragon? But are there such things as dragons today? Dr. Walter Auffenberg of the University of Florida knows there are.

Dr. Auffenberg and his fellow scientists are herpetologists—people who study reptiles and amphibians. Dr. Auffenberg's interest is the study of one group of lizards. This group is called the monitors, and includes the largest lizards in the world.

And what was the creature that Dr. Auffenberg met on the trail in the paragraph above? Why, none other than the Komodo dragon lizard! The Komodo dragon is the largest living monitor, spanning ten feet (3 meters) from snout to tail. No wonder the doctor was careful to stay out of its way!

The giant lizards living today can be traced back about 130 million years. They seem to have come from a family of now-extinct lizards called mosasaurs. Mosasaurs were water lizards whose bodies were well-suited to life in the sea. Their flat tails and paddle-like feet made them excellent swimmers. Their long jaws and sharp, curved teeth made catching fish an easy task. Some of the mosasaurs were more than 30 feet (9 m) long! It's a fact that the giant lizards of today had giants in their family tree.

The biggest mosasaur was Megalania. It is thought to have lived in what is now Australia more than a million years ago. The first fossil mosasaur was discovered in 1780 in Maastricht, a town in what was then the Spanish Netherlands.

The monitor lizards of today have the same ancestors as snakes. Most herpetologists agree that the forked tongue and movable lower jaw of the monitor make it a snake relative. The monitor's quick, darting tongue is used in much the same way as a snake's, to pick up particles from the air or the ground. These are then passed to the smelling organ, called the "Jacobson's organ," in the roof of the mouth. Both the lizard and the snake "smell" what they have found with this organ.

There are about 31 types of monitor lizards known today. Of these, about 16 will reach the length of three feet (0.9 m) or more as adults. When you think that the average lizard measures only 4 to 12 inches (10 to 30 centimeters), the large monitors really are "giant lizards" in the reptile family.

Giant lizards grow much larger than ordinary lizards.

CHAPTER ONE:

Monitor lizards live in the warmer parts of Africa, Asia, the East Indies, and Australia. No monitors are native to North or South America.

Heat is especially important to monitors because they are "ectothermic" animals (cold-blooded animals whose bodies take on the same temperature as their surroundings). At night and on cool mornings, their body temperatures are low, and the monitors are relatively inactive. They must absorb enough heat from the sun to warm their bodies to their ideal temperatures, which vary from species to species. For this reason, monitor lizards are "diurnal." This means that they are busy during the day and sleep or rest at night. In cold seasons, monitors become inactive, much like a bear that hibernates through the winter.

Keen senses and special features

All monitors have excellent vision and a very keen sense of smell. Since their eyes are positioned on either side of the head, monitors do not have binocular vision like humans. They take cues from each eye

The claws of the African Nile monitor are long and sharp.

separately. Their eyesight is very good for detecting quick movements or food at a distance. Monitors usually locate prey visually before chasing it. But they can smell dead and decaying prey several miles away!

A monitor's legs are ideal for climbing, swimming, or running. Each of the monitor's four powerful legs ends in five clawed toes. The claws are long and curved, perfect for pinning down prey or fighting.

The claws are also useful in grasping the bark of a tree and pulling the lizard up and away from danger. A monitor's grasp is extremely strong. Herpetologists

Sherman and Madge Minton tell of a story they heard many years ago:

"Several times while we were in Asia we heard stories of monitors being used as living grappling hooks by burglars or by soldiers attacking walled villages. The lizard, with a rope tied around its body just in front of the hind legs, climbs up a wall. When it reaches the top, the burglar or soldier holding the rope gives a tug, the lizard digs in its claws and holds on, and the man pulls himself up on the rope!"

Although the Mintons could not confirm the story and suspected it might be a folk tale, they admitted that there was nothing impossible about the story. The monitors' strength is well-documented.

Monitors have tapered heads with ear openings at either side, long and slender necks, and movable eyelids. Their nasal openings may be at the front tip of the head or nearer to their eyes. Monitors have lungs, not gills, and so they must breathe air to fill their lungs. But the more aquatic monitors are able to remain submerged for fairly long periods of time. Scientists believe that they may be able to seal off their nasal openings to prevent water from entering. Many monitors escape from a fight or from human predators by diving into the water and swimming away underwater. One species, the Nile monitor, can remain underwater for as long as one hour!

The long, narrow head of a monitor looks fierce.

The water monitor spends much of its time around the water and is an excellent swimmer.

The movable jaws of a monitor let it swallow its prey whole.

Jaws and teeth

The jaws of a monitor are powerful, and when the lizard clamps down on something it hangs on fiercely. Both upper and lower jaws are movable. The lower jaw can be extended by means of the lizard's "hyoid apparatus" (expandable joints at the rear of the lower jaw). This gives the monitor a larger mouth cavity and lets it swallow its prey whole, like a snake.

The teeth are arranged in two rows, one on each of the movable jaws. A monitor's teeth are somewhat flat, curved back, and serrated like a knife. The monitor's teeth, combined with its sharp claws, make it a formidable predator. An animal lucky enough to escape from the jaws of a monitor may still die from the wounds inflicted by those sharp teeth.

Gray's monitor is the one exception to the rule. While all monitors are carnivores and eat meat, Gray's monitor has a diet high in fruit and tree snails. Its rounded, peg-like teeth are better suited to its special diet.

Even though they have powerful jaws and teeth, monitors do not make many sounds. Most of the sounds they produce are not vocalizations. For instance, when monitors eat, they frequently sneeze to remove fly larvae from their nasal passages. A male may scratch his claws on the female's scales during courtship. Perhaps the only significant sound a monitor makes is its fearsome hissing, which is common in displays of aggression.

Scales cover the monitor

The body of a monitor is covered with small scales that do not overlap. Scales help reduce water loss, and let the monitor absorb heat from the sun. The scaly skin is thick and tough and acts like a suit of armor. Monitors have small, grainy scales over most of their

The tail of some monitors grows longer than the monitor's body.

bodies. Spiny scales appear in selected places for added protection, such as around the anal opening and on the head and neck.

New scales are formed by the tissues underlying the lizard's existing scales. When the new scales are fully formed, lizards shed their old skin.

Young monitors have more brightly colored scales which grow duller as the animals grow older. The bright colors may help to conceal the young that spend most of their time in the tree limbs of their habitats.

Adult monitors vary in color. Komodo dragons are grey-brown with red circles over their entire body. The two-banded water monitor is brown to black with yellowish bands above, and white or cream-colored below. The Australian Perenty has an ivory-colored neck with a coarse black network pattern over the rest of its body. The markings of the Nile monitor consist of yellow bands and spots on a greenish background. The Lace monitor is typically blue-black above with scattered white or yellow on the body, tail, and limbs.

Useful tails

In general, the tail of a monitor is thick and long (often more than half the total body length). The short-tailed monitor is the exception.

A few smaller monitors have prehensile tails. These tails grasp tree branches and wrap around them, enabling the monitors to move from tree to tree. The giant lizards, however, do not have prehensile tails. They spend their time on the ground or in the water, where their tails are used primarily for balance, defense, and as a rudder in swimming. They can also injure small prey with one swipe of their tail.

Scientists have noted that a monitor does not have the ability to regrow its tail as the smaller lizards do. A fight sometimes results in a monitor losing part of its tail. The lost part does not grow back.

Size and life expectancy

Monitors vary in size and weight. The smallest is the short-tailed monitor, which is eight inches (20 cm) long and weighs just a few ounces. The giant lizards are those that grow to at least three feet (0.9 m) long.

The real "stars" of the monitor family are: the Komodo dragon, which is ten feet (3 m) long and weighs up to 350 pounds (158 kilograms); the two-banded water monitor, which is eight to nine feet (2.4 to 2.7 m) long; the Perenty at seven feet (2.1 m) long; and the Lace Monitor and Nile monitor, both measuring six feet (1.8 m) long.

Many things affect the lifespan of a monitor. The food supply, the presence of predators (usually man), and injuries received in the wild can all make a difference in how long a monitor lives.

Individual monitors that have been studied have lived 15 or more years. However, some scientists think that under ideal conditions monitors might live 100 years.

The Australian goanna can grow to four feet in length!

CHAPTER TWO:

In 1982, Australian engineer Keith Steward made an unusual friend. While on a camping trip to Umbrawarra in the Australian outback, Stewart met a "goanna" (the Australian term for monitor lizard). This goanna was over four feet (1.2 m) long and lived in the deep green pools of a gorge where Stewart had set up camp.

The goanna who lived to eat

Stewart playfully named the goanna Cedric. Cedric was probably a Spencer's monitor, because it had brown coloring on its scales and a yellow neck. A Spencer's monitor can be any color from pale dirty cream to darker rusty brown, with scattered brown and cream spots. There may be irregular light yellow or grey cross bands on the neck, body, and tail.

The nostrils of a Spencer's monitor are positioned near the tip of the snout and off to each side. The tail is more or less round at its base (where it joins the body), but at its end it is compressed to resemble the keel of a boat. And, in fact, this monitor is an excellent swimmer.

Stewart was amazed at the monitor's great appetite and his eating habits. Here is an entry from Stewart's journal:

"Cedric came out again today. I caught three fish for him, two of which he devoured in front of me. The third, being considerably larger, put up such a fight that Cedric needed all his strength just to keep its head in his mouth. He persevered, however, throwing his entire body into the struggle, arching his neck stiffly and pressing the tail of the fish hard against the ground.

"His elastic reptile jaws opened wide, and he

A patient goanna waits for its next meal.

swallowed the entire fish. It took three or four minutes for him to force it down, during which time his body underwent amazing contortions. His neck must have swelled to twice its normal size as the head of the fish passed through. When the last of the tail was gone, Cedric opened his mouth wide, seeming to yawn for a moment, then turned back into the water and swam away."

Waiting for prey

A monitor will sit and wait for its prey to come within attack distance. For a Komodo dragon, this distance is between three and four feet (0.9 and 1.2 m).

The monitor then lunges forward suddenly and grabs whatever part of the animal's body it can. It clamps down with its sharp, serrated teeth and hangs on while the animal twists and turns, trying to free itself. This struggle often leads to the death of the prey. The monitor's teeth may cut through blood vessels and bones, crippling the captured animal.

Monitors have been known to catch and kill animals even larger than themselves. This means the monitor may be dragged a short distance before its prey gives up.

Even animals that manage to escape from the monitor's grasp are generally doomed, however. The bacteria in the monitor's mouth will eventually cause

Komodo dragons, like other monitors, will wait for hours until prey is within attack distance.

blood poisoning in the animal that has been bitten. The escaping prey may bleed to death or die from an infection.

Swallowing the meal

Monitors, like snakes, swallow their prey whole when they can. If the prey is too large to swallow

The scales of a Lace monitor are blue-black and speckled with yellow.

whole, the monitor's sharp teeth can usually crush the bones of its victim, and the monitor's powerful forelegs and claws make short work of breaking up the prey into manageable pieces.

Saliva begins to break down the monitor's food as soon as it enters the mouth cavity. A monitor's mouth has a strong bony roof that protects the mouth from damage while eating those large mouthfuls. The elongated, S-shaped necks of monitors can swell to make room for very large prey, as can their abdomens. Often, after feeding, a monitor's belly will hang down to the ground.

Some unpleasant habits

Since they are carnivores, monitors will eat any animal that lives in their habitat. Most of these lizards are also very fond of eggs, and will steal them from birds' nests, other lizards, and even a farmer's

Eggs are one of the monitor's favorite meals.

henhouse if they can get away with it. The Nile monitor is known to steal crocodile eggs, although these are usually closely guarded by the mother!

The monitor is very much aware of other animals' behavior patterns. It will wait for hours for the moment when the adult animal leaves its eggs in search of food. Even humans leave a henhouse unattended sooner or later, and that's when the monitor will seize its opportunity. Many researchers have reported that their tents were all but destroyed by hungry monitors tearing through baskets and backpacks in search of food.

The large monitors also feed on crustaceans, fish, frogs, snakes, rats, and birds. Monitors often eat the remains of another animal's kill (carrion). They can detect carrion by smell, even over long distances.

Watching giant lizards eat is not always a pretty sight. Dr. Auffenberg had many chances to observe Komodo dragons eating both carrion and live prey. He writes:

"I have observed one lizard gulp down the entire head of a wild boar; and in another instance we watched Number 28, a female weighing 110 pounds, devour 90 pounds of hog in 17 minutes!"

Dr. Wilbert Neugebauer of the Wilhelmina Zoo in Germany observed that, after eating, a monitor will lick its snout with its tongue, rub the sides of its head against the ground, and raise its head and look about. This appears to be an example of ritual behavior

When a monitor is hungry—watch out!

(behavior that is done automatically at specific times). It may signal to smaller lizards that they may now approach the remains of the kill and eat without fear of attack.

Smaller monitors and young monitors often instinctively roll around in the hair and intestines of carrion. Herpetologists believe this behavior protects them from being eaten by the larger monitors. Since monitors do not eat the intestines or hair of their prey, these odors on the smaller monitors keep the larger lizards away and thereby protect the smaller ones from attack.

In their role as scavengers, monitors help to clean up the environment by eating dead and decaying animal matter. They can make a meal out of "leftovers" that another predator leaves behind. This means that the monitor does not need to kill as often as an animal that does not eat carrion.

Dr. Auffenberg points out that monitors only kill when hungry. Because they need to conserve body heat by conserving energy, monitors are less likely to kill more prey than they can eat. And monitors save what they don't finish and eat it at the next meal.

Why cannibalism?

Reptiles are a lower (more primitive) form of life than mammals. They do not have a family life as wolves or elephants do. Furthermore, young lizards are not born helpless or dependent like wolf cubs or elephant calves are. Monitor lizards are able to live independently from the time they are hatched. So with no "family ties" to bind them (the lizard mother doesn't even know her own young since she leaves her eggs after depositing them), adults and hatchlings become competitors for the same food supply.

Although cannibalism, or the eating of their own kind, by adult monitors may seem cruel, the young are

Monitors do not have a family life; they live on their own as soon as they're born.

To avoid older monitors, young lizards hide in the treetops.

quite fast and equipped with many survival instincts such as keeping to the tree branches during non-feeding times. Only the weak or sick lizards are likely to be killed. In this way, these lizards are prevented from mating and the species is strengthened.

CHAPTER THREE:

The large monitor lizards live in various parts of the "Old World"—parts of Asia, Africa, and Australia.

Monitors are reptiles and must use the sun's rays to keep warm.

Being cold-blooded, they depend on a warm environment and the sun to raise their body temperatures after a cool night. Without such heat, monitors could not perform the basic activities of life. All monitors spend a good part of their day basking in the sun to absorb its heat.

Because of their sharp claws, small lizards and young monitors can climb trees and stay in the lower branches for a good part of the day. When they grow to adulthood, the monitors will take their places in the water, the desert, the plains, or the jungle. Each species of monitor has a very specific habitat.

The Komodo dragon makes its home on the island of Komodo, the tiny islands of Rintja and Padar, and a small part of western Flores in the Sunda Islands of Indonesia. Dragons sleep and take shelter under thick vegetation or in burrows they dig themselves.

The two-banded water monitor ranges from Ceylon and the southern part of India to China, the Philippines, and many Indonesian islands. It, too, finds shelter under vegetation and in crevices near the water. The water monitor is probably the most aquatic of monitor lizards. It spends much of its time in the water and is an excellent swimmer.

Another fine swimmer is the Nile monitor, found in Africa south of the Sahara Desert and as far south as the Cape of Good Hope. Although it prefers to live near the water, the Nile monitor can be found in nearly all parts of Africa except the desert.

Of the 31 species of monitors currently known, 16 can be found in Australia. The largest of these are the Perenty and the Lace monitors. The Perenty lives in desert areas where it prefers to hide in rock crevices. The Lace monitor is a tree lizard, so it is found in those habitats where the Perenty does not live: green, brush- and tree-covered territory. The Lace monitor, though large, is quite slender, so it can move through the trees with ease, unlike most adult monitors.

Unlike larger monitors, the Lace monitor can climb trees quickly and easily.

CHAPTER FOUR:

Courtship, mating, and young

Herpetologists have had difficulty observing the mating habits of monitors. There does not seem to be an elaborate courtship ritual as in some other animal species. Dr. Auffenberg notes that Komodo dragons will not mate with unfamiliar lizards just "passing through" their territory. But monitors do not develop lifelong attachments to a single mate, as geese, for example, do.

The male monitor signals his intention to mate by pursuing the female while making zigzag movements with his head. The male then grasps the female by the skin of the head or neck, pushes his tail under hers and twists his body to bring their cloacae (reproductive cavities) together. The male deposits the sperm that will fertilize the female's eggs.

Mating usually occurs in the spring. Monitors are egg-layers, so the female will deposit her eggs in a burrow or tree hollow. Hatching time varies among the species, with the largest monitors laying the largest eggs and requiring the longest hatching time

A monitor keeps a careful lookout for danger.

(approximately eight months for Komodo dragons).

Most monitor eggs are soft and leathery, not hard-shelled. The hatchlings bite through the egg with an "egg tooth" that protrudes from their snouts. The egg tooth is a real tooth that falls out soon after hatching.

One fact that interests herpetologists is that the Nile monitors and Lace monitors lay their eggs in termite mounds! By coincidence, the temperature and humidity in a termite mound are ideal for incubating the eggs. For some reason which scientists do not yet

Young monitors move quickly and easily from branch to branch.

understand, the termites do not disturb the lizard eggs. As soon as they hatch, the young lizards scurry out of the mound.

The largest monitors lay the fewest eggs at one time, sometimes as few as seven eggs in a clutch. Smaller monitors may deposit as many as 34 eggs at one time. When hatchlings finally arrive, they have no mother to care for them, since monitors do not rear their young. The young monitors will take to the trees for the first year of life. Otherwise, they may find themselves on the menu for any adult monitors in the vicinity.

CHAPTER FIVE:

Monitors are not social creatures. Although a male monitor will only mate with a female in his territory, they do not cooperate in food gathering or other daily life activities. Monitors may share carrion among themselves, but they have also been known to fight over food, territory, and mates.

Battles may lead to death

With their sharp teeth and claws, monitors are well-equipped to do battle with other animals or with each other. Dr. Neugebauer describes what happens when monitors fight each other:

"In male rivalry fights, the combatants are more restrained and generally do not use their teeth, claws, or tail. Each male stands up on its hind legs, and they face each other. Each attempts to push its opponent over, either to the side or backward. The goal here is to subdue the opponent and not to kill him... Competition over food is another matter, and fights here can result in bloody injuries."

The "crazy" monitor

Although most monitors do not attack humans unless cornered or provoked, there are exceptions to this rule, too. The dragon described in the opening chapter of this book was well known to Dr. Auffenberg. The dragon was thought to have been responsible for the death of one man whose body was found in the center of the lizard's home range. The lizard was called "ora gila"—the crazy Komodo monitor—by the native people. "I don't know if we could say he was 'crazy,' " says Dr. Auffenberg, "but he certainly was not normal. Perhaps he had been out in the sun too long. In any case, he was a lizard to be respected."

Dr. Auffenberg's research group learned of several

When monitors fight, they stand on their hind legs and try to push their opponent down.

attacks and at least one killing of natives by Komodo dragons. But much more common were lizard attacks on other animals.

Not man's best friend

Although only the Komodo dragons have attacked and killed humans, the personalities of other monitors are not much sweeter. Herpetologists find that most monitor lizards are aggressive, hyperactive, and unpredictable. Most researchers have teeth marks on their fingers or legs to prove it!

Monitors are evidently not afraid of the scent of human beings. When natives or visiting scientists leave their quarters, they often return to find that supplies have been ransacked. Domestic animals on local farms are not safe either.

Some monitors have been tamed, however. In zoos they quickly learn to recognize their keepers, answer to their names, and find their way around their new environments. Even in the wild, some researchers have made "pets" of monitors they were studying. One lizard was often known to go swimming with its human "friend." But monitors are wild animals, and any "friendships" they make take a back seat to their empty stomachs. As Keith Stewart learned when his "friend" Cedric bit him on the thumb, man's best friend is probably still his dog!

CHAPTER SIX:

The monitor has been linked to stories and beliefs that simply aren't true. For example, Egyptian folklore says that the monitor sucks milk from sheep and goats and is therefore bad luck for the shepherd. Some Malaysians believe that when crocodile eggs hatch, the female tries to eat all the young that run away from the water. The hatchlings that escape to the shore become monitor lizards. Still other people believe that if a monitor lizard is watching you and sees your teeth, you will be the victim of some terrible misfortune.

The most dangerous predator

The only serious predator that the giant lizards need to fear is man. Asian monitors have been used as food by man for centuries. They are killed for their meat and are used in soups and teas. Some superstitions make the monitors' body fat valuable in medicines. The fat is said to cure skin infections,

For extra protection, a monitor's scales can change color to match its surroundings.

arthritis, rheumatism, and even poor eyesight. Young monitors are used in a mixture of herbs, spices, and alcohol and sold as a tonic for the young and the very old to drink.

In Asia, the fashion industry uses lizard hides to make purses, belts, wallets, and shoes. Some tribal groups still use monitor lizard skins to make ceremonial drums and other musical instruments. Stuffed monitors with eyes made out of marbles are sold by the thousands as souvenirs.

The Komodo dragon is losing its natural prey—hog deer and wild boar—to local hunters. Soon, there may not be enough wildlife on the dragons' islands to sustain the population.

All monitor lizards are considered endangered species (in danger of extinction), but the giant lizards in particular need protection. These sometimes beautiful, often mysterious creatures may disappear if not fully protected. Breeding monitors in captivity is a tricky business. The giant lizards require large territories, specific diets, and controlled temperatures to breed successfully. Even zoos with experienced herpetology experts have not always had good luck breeding monitors. If the giant lizards become extinct someday—as well they might—the world will be a much less interesting place.

MAP:

■ Most monitors live within these areas.

INDEX/GLOSSARY:

AMPHIBIAN 5—*An animal that lives on land and in water but cannot breathe underwater.*

AQUATIC 10, 32—*Living in or near water.*

BINOCULAR VISION 8—*Using both eyes at once.*

CANNIBALISM 28—*Eating of one's own kind. Larger monitor lizards sometimes eat smaller and sicker lizards.*

CARNIVORE 15, 25—*An animal that feeds mainly on meat.*

CARRION 26, 27, 28, 37—*A dead and decaying animal.*

CLUTCH 37—*A nest of lizard eggs.*

DIURNAL 8—*An animal that is active only during the day.*

ECTOTHERMIC 8—*A cold-blooded animal with a body temperature that changes according to the temperature of the surroundings.*

EGG TOOTH 35—*A sharp tooth on the head of young reptiles used to help them escape from their shells. The tooth falls off after hatching.*

ENDANGERED 44—*An animal that is in danger of becoming extinct.*

EXTINCT 5, 44—*The loss of an animal species when the last member dies.*

FOSSIL 6—*The hardened remains or traces of an animal or plant from a former age.*

GOANNA 20—*The Australian term for monitor lizard.*

HABITAT 17, 25, 31, 32,—*The place where an animal makes its home.*

HATCHLINGS 35, 37, 41—*Young reptiles that hatch from eggs.*

HERPETOLOGIST 5, 6, 9, 27, 34, 35, 40, 44—*A scientist who studies reptiles and amphibians.*

INSTINCT 27, 30—*A natural behavior animals have from birth; it tells them what to do without their having to think about it.*

JACOBSON'S ORGAN 6—*The organ in the roof of a lizard's mouth that helps lizards smell.*

MOSASAUR 5, 6—*A prehistoric marine lizard that sometimes reached 40 feet (12 m) in length.*

ORA GILA 38—*The name given to Komodo dragon lizards by the natives who inhabit the islands where the lizards live.*

INDEX/GLOSSARY:

PREDATOR 10, 15, 18, 28, 41— *An animal that lives by preying on other animals.*

PREHENSILE TAIL 17, 18—*A lizard's tail that is adapted to grasping, holding, or wrapping around something.*

REPTILE 5, 6, 21—*A class of cold-blooded animals with a backbone. They breathe by means of lungs and usually have skin covered with horny plates or scales.*

RITUAL 26, 34—*A series of instinctive behaviors in animals that signal a specific response from other animals of the same species.*

SCAVENGER 28—*An animal that lives by feeding on the carcasses of animals killed by other predators.*

SERRATED 15, 22—*Notched like the edge of a saw.*

READ AND ENJOY THE SERIES:

If you would like to know more about all kinds of wildlife, you should take a look at the other books in this series.

You'll find books on bald eagles and other birds. Books on alligators and other reptiles. There are books about deer and other big-game animals. And there are books about sharks and other creatures that live in the ocean.

In all of the books you will learn that life in the wild is not easy. But you will also learn what people can do to help wildlife survive. So read on!